Growing Readers

Purchased with Smart Start Funds

FIRE STATIONS

GREAT PLACES TO VISIT

Jason Cooper

The Rourke Corporation
Vero Beach, Florida 32964

201 CHESTNUT STREET
WILMINGTON, N C 28401

Edited by Sandra A. Robinson

PHOTO CREDITS
© Lynn M. Stone: All photos

ACKNOWLEDGEMENTS
The author thanks the following for their cooperation in the preparation of this book: City of Aurora, IL, Fire Department; City of Batavia, IL, Fire Department; Tri-Com Central Dispatch, Geneva, IL

LIBRARY OF CONGRESS
Library of Congress Cataloging-in-Publication Data

Cooper, Jason, 1942-
  Fire stations / by Jason Cooper.
  p. cm. — (Great places to visit)
  Includes index.
  Summary: Examines the work, equipment, and personnel of fire stations.
  ISBN 0-86593-210-7

  1. Fire stations—Juvenile literature. 2. Fire extinction—Juvenile literature. [1. Fire departments. 2. Fire extinction.] I. Title. II. Series: Cooper, Jason, 1942- Great places to visit.
TH9148.C63 1992
628.9'25—dc20   92-8676
                                                     CIP
                                                     AC

Printed in the USA

TABLE OF CONTENTS

FIRE STATIONS

Fire fighters and shiny fire-fighting vehicles race to fires. When the fire has been put out, they return to a fire station, or firehouse.

The fire station is a garage for the fire trucks. It is also a house for the fire fighters of a fire department while they are on duty.

Fire station is both garage and home

KINDS OF FIRE STATIONS

Most fire departments and fire stations are run by cities and towns. Each fire station may have several fire-fighting vehicles and fire fighters. Most of the fire fighters work full-time at their job.

In small towns, the fire station may have only one fire truck or fire engine. The fire department in a small town may have to count on the help of **volunteer** fire fighters.

Volunteers have other jobs, but they become fire fighters when the fire alarm sounds.

6

Fire fighter in full dress

LIFE IN THE FIRE STATION

Fire fighters in city fire stations usually work a full, 24-hour day. At night they sleep in the fire station, unless the fire alarm sounds.

During the day, fire fighters stay busy in many ways when they are not fighting fires. One of their jobs is to keep the fire-fighting vehicles in perfect running condition.

Visitor finds fire engine in perfect condition

FIRE FIGHTERS

The fire fighters you meet on your visit are highly trained men and women. They are skilled at giving first aid to injured people as well as fighting fires.

Fire fighters visit schools, factories and homes. They try to find fire **hazards**—things that could cause fires—and remove them. They also help enforce fire safety laws.

A 911 dispatch office

Some of the fire fighter's basic equipment for fire fighting

FIRE SAFETY

Fire fighters talk about fire safety because it is so important. Fire fighters remind young people that in most cities they can report a fire by dialing 911 on a telephone.

Each year about 6,000 people in the United States die in fires. Dozens of fire fighters die, too, helping to rescue people and put out fires. Fire fighting is one of the most dangerous jobs in the world.

FIRE-FIGHTING VEHICLES

You will see many kinds of fire-fighting vehicles. Some are known as fire trucks. Others are called fire engines. Many of these vehicles are made specially for a particular city's needs.

Fire-fighting vehicles of one kind or another carry water, pumps, hoses and ladders. Ladder trucks are sometimes equipped with a ladder that cranks out over 100 feet—longer than a basketball court!

Ladder truck extending a small part of its 100-foot ladder

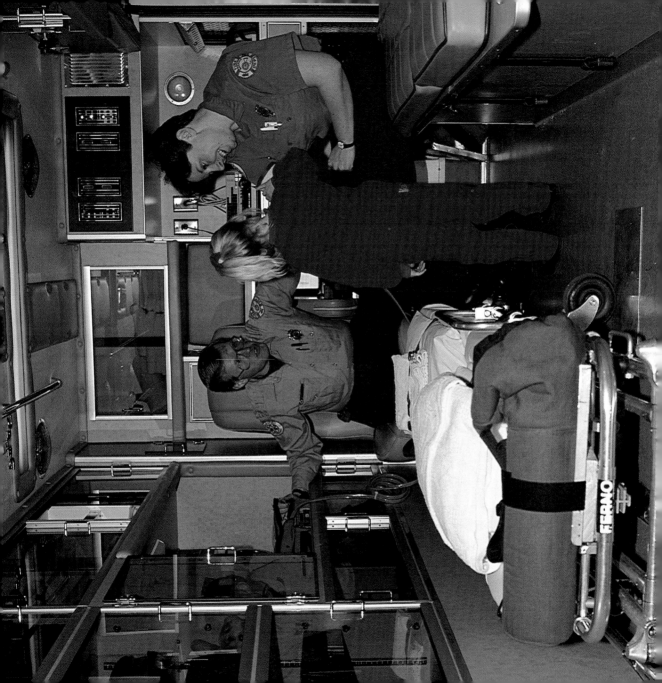

RESCUE TRUCKS

Fire stations have vehicles that are used to help people—ambulances and rescue trucks. People called **paramedics,** some of whom are also fire fighters, operate the ambulance. Paramedics are trained to aid people who are badly hurt in fires and accidents.

A rescue truck has fire-fighting equipment and special equipment to help free people from wreckage in an accident.

Paramedics in a rescue vehicle with young visitor

FIRE!

Most fire stations are alerted to a fire by a **dispatch** office. Calls to report a fire ring in the dispatch office first.

Fire fighters rush to their coats, boots and helmets. Fire fighters who may be upstairs save time by sliding down a metal pole to their vehicles. In seconds, fire fighters and their vehicles are roaring to the fire.

Brass fire pole saves precious seconds when alarm sounds

FIRE-FIGHTING EQUIPMENT

Look closely at the fire fighter's weapons against fire. Most fire fighters' gear includes a helmet, coat, gloves, flashlight, mask and radio. He or she may also carry a tank of fresh air to breathe and other safety items.

The fire fighter has **fire extinguishers,** axes, ropes and many other helpful objects available on the truck. But fire fighters know that their greatest weapon against fires is prevention—stopping a fire *before* it starts.

Glossary

dispatch (DIS patsh) — a message

fire extinguisher (FIRE ex TIN gwish er) — a container that holds a substance used to put out, or extinguish, fires

hazard (HAZ erd) — something that is a danger

paramedic (pair uh MEHD ik) — someone who is trained to care for seriously injured people before they reach a doctor's care

volunteer (vohl un TEER) — someone who freely does a job without being paid for it

23

INDEX